the ground beneath my feet

J. R. Darbon

J. R. Darbon

Copyright © 2020 *the ground beneath my feet*

written by J R Darbon
@jrdarbon

cover art by Johnny Redford
@johnnyrart

ISBN: 9798686284098

the ground beneath my feet

the ground beneath my feet © 2020
by J. R. Darbon

All rights reserved. No part of this book may be reproduced or used in any manner without written permission from the copyright owner except for the use of questions in a book review.

Kindle Direct Publishing

J. R. Darbon

the ground beneath my feet

Chapter 1… the love i give
Chapter 2… the pain i feel
Chapter 3… the value i hold

J. R. Darbon

the ground beneath my feet

to all the people part of my story; words will never be able to describe how much you all mean to me.

i cannot begin to thank you enough, for the poetry, for the words, for the memories. to my closest friends, the ones who know the stories, the ones who have both cried and laughed with me, thank you. thank you, for everything you helped me read, feel and write.

J. R. Darbon

the ground beneath my feet

Chapter 1

the love i give

J. R. Darbon

the ground beneath my feet

nothing ever felt more like love, than the
tips of my fingers gliding over the
goosebumps on your back.

J. R. Darbon

time stood still the night we first met,
laying on the top of a London hill in the
peak of summer at midnight. the humid
air kept us afloat, above the crisp dry grass
where our fingers wrapped around one
another, staring at the stars glistening
above us.

that's Cygnus he said softly, as he began
to mirror the pattern across my forearm.
he continued, each star represents a point
in a journey, a connection made worth
holding onto, as the goosebumps on my
skin mimicked the sky in which he
traced. we gazed upwards, longingly,
both silently knowing that this was the
first connection in our journey; the
constellation of us.

the ground beneath my feet

even with your eyes half open and your
torso draped on mine sweaty from the
night, i had never felt love so pure.

J. R. Darbon

he asked me if i wrote poetry, whilst his fingers echoed chills along my spine. my breath deepened as i paused for a moment, anticipation surging through my veins, locking glistening eyes, slowly leaning in closer. i perched my teeth on his lower lip, pulling it away from his body gently. my hands lingered over his soft coffee stubble, feeling the clench of his jaw. i don't just write it, i whispered, i make it.

the ground beneath my feet

there are so many places on this earth i
dream of being, but none more than
entwined with you.

J. R. Darbon

we walked side by side under the luminous moon, whilst the soft breeze lightly swayed the trees beside us. his hand reached out for mine, pulling my body closer. we paused for a moment, as if the world had stopped spinning, our fingers still entangled between one another, looking upwards at the midnight sky. our breath synchronising with the collapsing of the waves. switching his focus to my eyes he resumed his longing gaze. it's beautiful isn't it he remarked. almost as beautiful as you.

the ground beneath my feet

sometimes we talk about things that are surreal to me, like astrology and the stars. you love the idea of the universe, the stars, moon risings, planets and how they influence our world. sometimes i think you're crazy, but at midnight when i'm alone and looking out the window at the moonlit sky, i can't help but smile at it all, because i don't believe it's possible the universe didn't send you to me, to teach me, help me and love me. how could i disagree, when you are the moon to my tide pulling me in at night, holding me tightly, loving me like the shore.

J. R. Darbon

the sun on my skin and his hand in mine.
                         that's all i need.

the ground beneath my feet

in silent midnight conversations with the
stars, i tell them about your eyes. they listen
in adulation, longing to shine the way yours
do. and as the moon moves across the sky,
the ground beneath my feet gently spinning,
i know just how envious they are,
of a love like ours.

J. R. Darbon

his eyes widened across the car holding my stare as i leant in towards him. my mouth softly outlining his, raising hairs on my neck. our lips gently dancing together, savouring every taste softly and slowly as the chills continued throughout my body. the night halted with my lips still rested on his. that was the moment i knew, he was the one for me.

the ground beneath my feet

i've never been good at loving anyone. it's taken a lot for me to love and be loved, my flaws and insecurities bubbling underneath. but between your eyes and mine lays the reason i no longer feel like that, the air between us is light and surrounding us is nothing but love. thank you for showing me what love is, without even saying a word.

i remember those long nights, we stayed up later than the stars. his coffee eyes and golden skin twinkling in the moonlight reflecting off the ocean like a kaleidoscope. deep blue jeans torn at the knees, and a plain white t-shirt clung to his body tightly. our souls taking flight, chasing the night as we sunk deeper into the sand. we didn't know what dawn held, as our time was now, to love and to be loved.

the ground beneath my feet

the gentle feel of your lips on mine as we lock limbs under the sheets, our tongues intertwining, bodies pressed together, hearts beating faster, our breath quickening, hands roaming softly upon the surface locking eyes for a moment falling back into a state of euphoria. that was the intimacy you taught me.

J. R. Darbon

isn't it amazing how easily you chased away
my demons, with just the feel of your lips,
the softness of your voice and the caress of
your hand on my body. then, suddenly, the
darkest parts of me could
breathe again.

the ground beneath my feet

you make me feel sexy he says, with a quiver of doubt in his voice. i stare and smile. if only you knew how much more than that i think you are.

J. R. Darbon

    his lips were pink, lined with soft brown stubble. the way they moved hypnotised me, the way they felt awoke my soul. i savoured every taste, every spine-chilling moment they spent dancing with mine, endlessly into the night.

the ground beneath my feet

i don't think i'll ever forget those nights
we'd lay under the summer's night sky. the
way your hand traced my body drawing the
constellations, freckle to freckle leading your
fingertips along my skin. i would look into
your eyes, the deepest shade of brown,
watching them lighten under the stars.
i never wanted those nights to end.

J. R. Darbon

and i had never seen a love as perfectly
blended as the sunset and the ocean, until
my body met yours.

the ground beneath my feet

fleeting moments of silence, alone together. the sun chasing freckles across his body as our torsos became familiar. locked lips releasing just as quickly as the breeze changed, thousands of moments passing, yet barely seconds together.

J. R. Darbon

salty air filled our lungs as the setting sun kissed our already golden skin from beyond the ocean. the placid breeze cooling my skin, as his hair lightly floated behind him to the sound of gentle waves kissing the shore. each step in the wet sand leaving a footprint behind the last. my heart smiled, knowing this was the happiness i had always dreamt about.

the ground beneath my feet

honey eyes, soft skin. sparks flying between our lips. hairs rising, clothes falling. i pull away for a moment holding his gaze. how badly do you want it? i whisper, keeping his body at arm's length. his honey eyes widen, a gentle smirk across his cupid bow lips. he takes my arm, locking his fingers into mine. mouth to mouth he softly says, almost as much as i want you.

J. R. Darbon

the sunlight reflecting in his hazel brown eyes reminded me of warmth. like coffee on a cold winter's day. staring blissfully in his gaze weightlessly bound to him. giving me everything i needed to start my day.

the ground beneath my feet

we laughed in the humid air on the beach as the night crept out of reach, with the sky slowly turning orange to welcome the sun. the chorus of birds beginning to wake softly singing a melody encouraging us to dance bare foot in the velvet sand, losing our balance, gripping to one another as we continued. i began to stumble on the uneven mounds, pulling his body to the floor. our chests pressed together lightly, still laughing as the tide approached us inquisitively. what the hell are we doing, he asked whilst smiling.

falling in love the way we should.

J. R. Darbon

Sunday mornings. awoken by his kiss as the light broke through the gaps in the curtain. we rose slowly, unravelling our bodies from one another. i would make us both a cup of coffee, the colour of his eyes whilst he cooked breakfast in his underwear, hair still messy and eyes adjusting to the day. sat at the table, my over shirt loosely hanging from one shoulder as i stretched my docile body. he would look at me, lovingly as i smiled back. neither of us needed to say a word; we both knew nothing would ever be as perfect, as Sunday mornings with us.

the ground beneath my feet

we stepped in on floor two, down in the elevator to floor one. a wasted journey i thought, the stairs would be much quicker. shut up and kiss me, i've been desperate to get you alone he said, barely finishing his sentence before his lips told mine the rest.

J. R. Darbon

love is not always beautiful; it can be messy, reckless, a hurricane of emotions. but even in the chaos of everything else around, i still found peace in your soul.

the ground beneath my feet

i want to stay under your skin where our love will last forever, under the covers you and i, safely together as one.

J. R. Darbon

show me you. the deepest. the darkest. the most insecure. the most vulnerable. share your pain. share with me your story. i want to know each and every part of who you are. i want to help you heal. and for what i cannot help you heal, i want to sit and hold you through. i want to be the one to show you that even within the darkness of your own mind, you can always find the light. i can't promise i'll know how to help you, but i promise i'll hold each part you show me more tenderly than the last.

the ground beneath my feet

if i could have one wish, it would be that kiss with you lasted a little longer.

J. R. Darbon

a loyal man with a kind heart,
honest eyes and a dirty mind.
              that's all i want.

the ground beneath my feet

treat me like a winter's night, hold me tight
and let me stay warm within your embrace,
      even if only till morning comes.

J. R. Darbon

just hold me tonight, safe in your arms. i'll be fine when the light of dawn breaks, but for now i need the solitude of your arms to make it all okay.

the ground beneath my feet

and i know you think loving you is difficult,
that you are too much sometimes. but loving
you is the easiest thing i could ever do.

you taught me so much about love. that intimacy was more than physical. that love was more than between the sheets, that it was more than simply spending time with someone. you showed me that love was the get home safe messages, the good morning texts, the random box of chocolates because you knew they were my favourite and saw them at the checkout. you taught me that love was turning a late-night trip to the supermarket into an adventure. that cold winter days were perfect for walks with cups of hot chocolate and that muddy clothes just meant we had all the more reason to get into pyjamas and cosy up on the sofa. but most of all, you taught me that love was real. and even though you also taught me that love does not always stay, you taught me that love does not have to be painful. so, for that, i will always have love for you.

the ground beneath my feet

i wonder if you ever think of me. i know
years have passed, but i still think of you.
you were my first love, the first man i ever
touched, the first to make me feel deeper
than just anybody could. those nights that
never seemed to end, enmeshed together on
sandy beaches, kissing to the sound of the
waves flirting with the shore.

i wonder if part of you still loves me.
because part of me still loves you.

J. R. Darbon

let's take our love back to the start. meet me
under the constellations to the east, where
our love first started, the night your soul
joined forces with mine.

the ground beneath my feet

the older i get, the more i realise love isn't what we think it is. it isn't the end scene of the movie, running through the airport. it isn't the expensive dinners, the gifts and the glamour we believe it to be. it's the random texts because they saw something and thought of you, the little notes left on the side, the morning laughs getting ready for work, the shoulder to cry on when you need it. love really is, in it's purest form, the simplicity of you and them and the connection you share.

J. R. Darbon

love may have been painful, but it has also been beautiful. do not allow the wounds you are healing to prevent you from moving forwards again. yes, love has hurt you deeply. but the scars you have gained have shown the strength of your soul. trust that love will not always be perfect, but it will be worthwhile. true love only comes if you allow yourself to embrace it again.

the ground beneath my feet

kindred souls will always find a way to be together, no matter how many obstacles they face. you might have mountains in your way, you may have to cross oceans, but it will all be worthwhile. it might seem like an impossible task, but believe me when i say; if it's meant to be, you will make the journey. you both will. i cannot promise there won't be hurdles, you may have to go off course, you may have to weather some storms. these are all vital to your story, because two souls in love will endeavour it all, to finally be together.

J. R. Darbon

being in love has far less to do with holding on to what you have and much more to do with developing what you could. love should not limit you, it should propel you constantly through time, each day stronger than the last.

the ground beneath my feet

and just like that, here i am.
falling again, with nothing to lose,
but everything to gain.

J. R. Darbon

please, if you believe anything i say, let it be this. someday, someone will come into your life and change it all. they will hold you so tightly yet softly that all your broken pieces heal back together. they will show you what love is supposed to be, how it is supposed to feel. you must believe me, your happily ever after is coming.

the ground beneath my feet

at the end of the day, i'm just glad i could make you happy. i'm glad i made you feel something not everyone else could. i'm glad i loved you the way i did. i know we weren't meant to last, we couldn't raise our voices louder than the thunder that raged between us, but i'm glad we at least danced in the rain together, even if only for a short song.

J. R. Darbon

somewhere along the road i think i stopped believing in love. i stopped believing in the genuine intentions of those i interacted with, second guessing their every move. having been a victim of false love before, i know the perils of giving yourself to somebody who only intends on hurting you. that was, until i met you.

the ground beneath my feet

i cannot wait for the day, i look into his eyes
and say i love you. i love you. i cannot wait
for the day i say i love you and truly, truly
mean it. with every fibre of my being, when
the 'i love you' means everything it is
supposed to and more, when i finally
understand the true value of
those three words.

J. R. Darbon

years later i still sit on that same beach,
wondering if you sat here next to me for the
first time, would we fall in love
all over again?

the ground beneath my feet

i yearn for a love so deep envy itself would cry. so please, if you ever find yourself stuck between choosing me or them. choose them.

J. R. Darbon

concern yourself with finding love in somebody who makes the mundane an adventure, that makes the early morning car journey's exciting. somebody who makes the boring dinners with smiley faces squirted in ketchup, just to make you laugh. these are the things that keep the love alive, so treasure the people who do these, because they are the ones that still make you smile, even when you cannot find the strength to yourself.

the ground beneath my feet

J. R. Darbon

the ground beneath my feet

Chapter 2

the pain i feel

J. R. Darbon

the ground beneath my feet

       his lips tasted like the sweetest poison, i loved nothing more than the way they burnt me. so soft yet so painful. his tongue the stirrer, mixing lies and the violence of his words into my blood stream with each kiss. each bite of my lip slightly harder than the last. just one more taste, how dangerous can it be.

J. R. Darbon

i had this fascination with mermaids i would often tell him about. how they would lay on the jagged rocks, basking in the glory of the sun on their scintillating skin, inveigling sailors in with their beauty. a false sense of comfort with an unknowing peril nearby. the sailors would go towards them full of desire, like i did him, unaware of the darkness that was hidden from sight. when they became just close enough to touch, the sirens would drag them under the depths of the water, changing their beauty for nefarious ways, laying the sailor to waste amongst the wreckage of their ship. leaving nothing but a broken vessel and a story only few would believe.

the ground beneath my feet

in that moment after the fight, when your
eyes held my glare, with lips perched on
mine, i forgot how badly you'd ever hurt
me. and once again,
i was yours.

J. R. Darbon

i tilt my head back to stop the outpour of waves, hoping to drown my eyes in their own salty pools of pain and emotion. maybe that way i'll stop seeing him in everything i do.

the ground beneath my feet

i let you break me into a thousand pieces
in the hope that you would call
at least one of them yours.

J. R. Darbon

do you know how numbing it feels to not feel like you are enough. shout every word of praise my way. bask me in the glory of your words. but if you are not putting my body on that same pedestal with your actions, i'll never feel like i've won.

the ground beneath my feet

i mistook the red flags for butterflies, fell for words over actions, believed i was building him, when i was only breaking myself.

9:15pm.
i sit down on the sofa. he walks out the
door. i sip my wine, his favourite.
i spit it from my mouth with
venom as if it were poison.
scratch my eyes.
lunge across the room attacking
the photographs of he and i.
the broken frames slash my fingers.
i tear the watch he bought from my wrist,
hurling it across the room,
hoping it would break.
i look up at the photograph in the hallway
and crash to the ground.
blood screams from my fingertips
as i cradle myself.
tears flooding out of my eyes.
the watch lay smashed but ticking.
photos intact outside the frame.
the bottle of wine still half full.
how is it only me in this moment,
who is completely broken.
9:17pm

the ground beneath my feet

i hate that you still have a hold over me. i hate that your name still rings alarm bells in my mind, all this time later. i hate that you haven't spoken to me in two years, yet i still hear your last words rattling through my mind. i hate that when i lay with him, i think of you. i hate that when i wake up, for that split unconscious second i think it's going to be your body entwined with mine. i hate that when my phone rings from a +44 number i read it first hoping it's you. i hate that i have your number memorised, but not saved. i hate that you loved me so hard and i did you. i hate that i don't hate you, in fact, i know we never said this, but i hate that i love you, still, after all this time. but most of all, i hate that i know if you stood before me right now, asking for it all again, i'd say no. because there are still too many fragments of glass pierced into my skin from the day i left, to ever fully heal from you.

you shouldn't go to war for a love that wouldn't fight for you. i know how hard you want to, but this relationship is no longer serving you. when the battles you face cause more damage than they resolve, you must put down your weapons. sometimes the most worthwhile fight is the one with yourself, the one that gives you the feeling you deserve.

the ground beneath my feet

just because you love them,
does not mean you should stay.

J. R. Darbon

i hate to break it to you, but if he loved you, he wouldn't make you feel this way. he wouldn't make you feel insecure, he would listen to you and be honest. he would reassure you truthfully, honestly. he would make sure you were okay. but he isn't. he doesn't and truly, he never did. if he loved you, he would make sure you never had to question it, because true love should not leave you half empty, it should leave you overflowing.

the ground beneath my feet

i remember saying i love you, but now i realise that wasn't love. he was never the love of my life i believed him to be. he kept too many secrets, too many skeletons in the closet. you cannot give all of yourself to somebody and receive half in return, that is not love. the man i loved was a mirage, a false sense of hope in a barren land. and that is not a love i ever want to stand by.

J. R. Darbon

it hurt a lot less letting go,
than it did accepting a shackled love
from you.

the ground beneath my feet

he was an actor, scripting our story. he chose
the villains, giving himself the hero role. he
directed it all, the manipulation of emotions
whilst he played the favoured part. he would
cut scenes, avoiding himself being seen in a
negative light, playing me off as the one who
needed saving. the worst of it all was
realising none of it was real to him, it was all
part of the perfect drama he'd written for us,
in his fantasy world of lies.

i loved you for who you pretended to be.

the ground beneath my feet

the way they speak to you tells you everything. you're too clingy to somebody who doesn't want you to touch them. to needy to somebody who doesn't want to talk. too emotional to somebody who doesn't want a deeper connection with you. pay attention to their words, they'll tell you everything you need to know.

J. R. Darbon

the peter pan role wears thin after a while; boys that don't grow up will never be men. the way he handles situations tells you everything. men own their mistakes; men take charge and make it right. boys run and cry, playing the blame game. that is the difference between the two.

the ground beneath my feet

let them lie about you. let them sow the seed of the person you are. let them change your narrative, let them paint you in villainous red. at the end of it all, the smoky mirrors they look at themselves through will be the ones that suffocate them, not you.

J. R. Darbon

i showed you parts of me you
did not deserve to see.

the ground beneath my feet

there are so many people worth loving,
why do you choose the ones who aren't?

J. R. Darbon

and you might love them, but do they make you love yourself?

the ground beneath my feet

you really don't know me. i have shed every
strand of who i was when you knew me. i'm
not that weak person you once controlled.
your manipulative words no longer swing a
pendulum in front of my eyes deceiving my
heart into believing fake love could
ever be true.

J. R. Darbon

it's amazing how one action can change
everything you thought you knew about
somebody. an outer body experience, exiling
all emotion out of your soul.
do you still love him?
they asked me.
every fibre of love left me, the moment
i knew the truth about him. do you hate
him? they repeated.
i paused. how can i hate somebody
i do not know.

the ground beneath my feet

i doused the memories in gasoline, lit the
match and watched them burn.

J. R. Darbon

every i love you reverberated through my ribs with the echo of broken promises, with the collapse of a forever that never came.

the ground beneath my feet

but that's it, isn't it. you etched pain into my skin and sold it to me for the high price of love. i was ready to lose myself to love you, i was prepared to give up on myself because you couldn't accept me to have my own mind, my own voice, my own story. the worst part is, you would have let me fall at your feet under the pain of your words and convince me it was love.

J. R. Darbon

there's no covering it in cotton wool - some people deserve what happens to them. softness is not a skill, it's a choice. the same way that cruelness is. so the next time somebody makes you feel less than worthy by choice, the next time somebody tries to break who you are; remember that the universe notices and repays them, in ways just as wicked as theirs.

the ground beneath my feet

that is the problem with broken boys; they pretend they are whole. but they are not. they scatter themselves thin between many beds, hoping to piece themselves together. they say words, so untrue from one to another that seem sincere, hopeful you might believe them. these boys know no remorse, lusting for the power of pain. they find strength in manipulating you into being their source of safety, only to chip away at your pieces, with the hope of fixing their broken parts.

J. R. Darbon

maybe i do live too fast, too dangerously, too wildly. maybe i am some of the things you said, too loud, too much, too out there and too chaotic. and maybe i am everything you begrudged, everything you resented and everything you envied. but i would rather be all of these things and more, than anything like you.

the ground beneath my feet

you can attack my character as much as you wish, you can lie to everyone about who i am, but you will never take me to the depths of pain you live in. and knowing that, means your words will never hurt me again.

J. R. Darbon

do not confuse my words. i write for me, not for you. i experienced heartbreak, but i am not heartbroken. i have felt insecure, but i am still confident. i fell, i broke, but i did not shatter. i healed. i grew. i learnt. so, the next time you read my words of pain, know each word took me higher than you would ever know.

the ground beneath my feet

i found peace with the apology i never received. frankly i didn't need it. the words of somebody so manipulative would have carried no genuine meaning either way.

J. R. Darbon

i knew it was over, the moment he didn't choose me. truthfully, he never chose me. not really. i wanted to believe he loved me, but simple actions never took off with the wind. maybe i liked being the one who loved so much more, perhaps his damaged soul gave me purpose, someone to help learn their potential. the truth is, i broke myself helping somebody that couldn't be helped. he didn't want to be better, he just wanted those highs in between it all. the quick fixes of attention, the sudden heights that led to desperate falls. and with that knowledge,
i became free.

the ground beneath my feet

our love ended the moment
the truth came out.
how could i love a man
i never truly knew?

J. R. Darbon

i cannot love somebody i do not respect;
that is what makes this so much easier.

the ground beneath my feet

if there is one thing i've learnt, it's that you must pay attention to the red flags. no matter how much you want to see past them or how into them you might be.

J. R. Darbon

wish on all the stars you like, the digits of the clock, the pennies in the well. you never could take responsibility for yourself could you, you never did favour action over words. you were always looking for something else to blame when things went wrong, maybe that's why you keep losing. the star passes by, the clock ticks on, the penny sinks to the bottom. yet here you are, thinking you can go on like this.

the ground beneath my feet

funny thing is, i did really love you. i loved you with everything i had, with every ounce of my being. but you didn't deserve to stay in my life, no matter how purely i felt. i didn't deserve to feel less than worthy, my love for myself would not allow it. so please know that i loved you and that will never change, but you are no longer welcome in the life that i've built from the ashes of the heart that you burnt down.

falling in love with potential is dangerous. this is not always equal to reality. you might think they can be this amazing person; you might want to do everything you can to help them achieve this. but make sure you're attentive to red flags, the way they react to you, the way they support you in return. because a person who is not ready to achieve their potential will only limit you from reaching yours.

the ground beneath my feet

thank you for showing me everything that
i do not wish to be. for showing me
everything that love is not. for showing me
everything, you could never be.

J. R. Darbon

you remind me a lot of tequila, once my
drink of choice, now i shudder at
the thought of you.

the ground beneath my feet

you were wrong about me. you told me i had so many issues, that i was damaged in so many ways. i almost believed it. but that was just another of your lies. i expressed my insecurities to have them contorted, twisted back into myself, piercing my skin and drawing blood from my own words. You made me feel as if i were weak for doubting your reply, when everything i questioned about you turned out to be true. you took my vulnerability and wrapped it round my throat, in the hope that i would kill myself before i realised who you really were.

J. R. Darbon

you're handling this well
they said.
i know my worth
i replied.

the ground beneath my feet

we did not work;
we were never able to balance night and day.
i loved you too much, that was my downfall.
you hated yourself too much,
that was yours.

thank you. thank you for all the pain you tried to cause me. thank you for all the lies you told. thank you for the mistreatment. thank you for stabbing me in the back. thank you for showing me my strength. thank you for teaching me my worth despite your every effort to reduce it. thank you for making me the person i am today, the person who will not back down. so thank you for all of your evil, because it only made me greater.

the ground beneath my feet

whatever is in my past is behind me.
i do not have ill will towards what i can
no longer see.

J. R. Darbon

loving you didn't teach me how to love someone right, walking away from you did.

the ground beneath my feet

forgiveness came to me one night, under the stars we used to wish on. none of it was real, he and i. all of it based on maybes and one days, the fickle concept of fate determining our lives as if we are not in control of our own actions, as if we do not bear the consequences of our choices. hidden behind a mask of fortune, true love could never be found and in that, i found my peace.

J. R. Darbon

you only realised the light in my eyes, after
they stopped shining around you, a few
broken promises too many,
a few tomorrows too late.

the ground beneath my feet

losing you was the beginning of
rediscovering me, the start of self-love that
had been so long overdue. i used to think
you broke me. but i was never broken, i was
simply lost. and now that i have found
myself, i'll never let go of who i am again.

maybe you are sorry. maybe you have changed. maybe you will be better. maybe you will love me right. but you lost that privilege the moment you treated me like i was disposable. you don't get to have me back after you so willingly discarded me, seeking greener pastures when mine were plentiful. you lost me. what part of that don't you understand? you hurt me more times than you made love to me, you cast me away when you decided i wasn't enough. so no, i don't care who you will be, how sorry you are or how you will love me. because i deserve so much better than somebody who so willingly walked away, only to realise they sold the home they were meant to spend the rest of their life in.

the ground beneath my feet

there's not a single thing you could do or
say, that would ever make me love you
again. and in that,
i have all the closure
i need.

J. R. Darbon

the ground beneath my feet

Chapter 3

the value i hold

J. R. Darbon

the ground beneath my feet

losing you wasn't much like losing, in fact, losing you was so much more like winning. the freedom to be me again, the adventure of finding who i am. leaving you taught me the kind of peace my soul desired, the kind of self-love my heart deserves.

J. R. Darbon

but whilst you were out searching for others to sleep in your bed, i was out building myself. so, don't be surprised when you see me alone and thriving, as you scatter yourself thin between each person, desperately trying to take pieces of them to make something of yourself.

the ground beneath my feet

if i'm being honest, i'm scared. i'm scared of being betrayed again, scared of giving myself to somebody who will break me. i'm scared of losing myself in the midst of it all. i'm scared of breaking what i've worked so hard to rebuild. but what i fear most is the fear itself holding me back from experiencing something great.

J. R. Darbon

close the door. you don't have to hate someone, to not want them coming and going from your life anymore. hold yourself higher than that, know that your world is more important, your self-esteem deserves more than someone who only wants to visit, but not stay.

the ground beneath my feet

you are not selfish for expressing your insecurities. you are not weak for having your doubts. you are not foolish if you lose. you are not unworthy if you struggle. anyone who makes you feel any of this, are these themselves.

J. R. Darbon

people in the modern day are too quick to dispose of one another, rather than grow together. not me. i'm not one to give up or throw things away easily. anything i've invested myself into emotionally will get my full attention, effort and soul to make it work. so, when i choose to walk away, do not take this lightly. because when i do leave, i know i'm never coming back.

the ground beneath my feet

seeing the goodness in somebody is not a weakness. staying when it gets tough, fighting for what you believe in is not a defect. but make sure the person you are doing this for is worthy of you, that they show you they appreciate you. because you have to fall in love with the person who proves they deserve you, through their light and their dark days as well as yours.

J. R. Darbon

this is the thing, i'm not ready. i'm not ready to be someone's person, i'm not ready to deal with the trials of a relationship. i refuse to break another person finding myself, lord knows i've been on the other side of that. i need to find myself, to root myself down and bloom into me, before i can look to appreciate the beauty of another.

the ground beneath my feet

you must find acceptance in yourself. chasing a reaction from them is not beneficial. they won't know what they've lost, because they didn't realise what they had. but when they do, you will be so far gone it will all be a distant memory. and in that, you must find peace.

J. R. Darbon

before there was an us, there was a me.
after us, there is still me.

the ground beneath my feet

this year has taken me to every limit thinkable. i have laid in the depths of hell yet found a way to appreciate the beauty of the flames that engulfed me. i have been spun fiercely in the tornado yet found peace within its eye. i have been bruised, beaten and broken, but healed each and every time. i have amazed myself with my resilience. i have stood tall amongst the wreckage of the elements, asking the lightning to strike me again, knowing that i didn't just ride the storm, i became it.

J. R. Darbon

i'd be lying if i said i wasn't still hurt, truth is i still feel the pain of every loss, every betrayal, of every goodbye. but i wouldn't change these experiences, they made me who i am. they reminded me of my worth, of my future and have taught me more than i could have ever imagined.

the ground beneath my feet

stop shaming yourself for not fitting the mould others make you believe you should fit. one person's failure is another's success, one person's one day is somebody else's yesterday. stop dictating your life based on the perception others have of you, the perception you have of yourself. at the end of the day, when you are grey and old, reminiscing on your life, you won't talk about how you were the top of the pecking order in your office by 30, how you had the perfect body from hours in the gym, how straight your smile was or how you earnt a 6 figure salary. you'll talk about your life, the people you loved, the places you visited, the things that still make you laugh 60 years after they happened. so, worry less about where you are and what others think of you, because at the end of it all, the only person who knows how happy you are is you. and once you're gone, the only people who'll know how happy you were, will be those you convinced to live their lives, just as purposefully as you lived yours.

J. R. Darbon

i'm done faking it, pretending, doing anything to fit in. i know who i am, what i want and what i expect. i refuse to compromise myself for anything, it took too long to love the person in the mirror to be anything but authentically me.

the ground beneath my feet

you know, truly all you need is a handful of friends around you. the ones who can pick you out of the broken glass when you want it all to end without passing judgement. the ones who cry along with you because they feel your pain. the ones who can make you laugh so powerfully it hurts. the ones who adventure with you, holding memories just as close as you do. the ones who honestly care; the ones who love you as much as you love them.

J. R. Darbon

even when you are walking through the fire,
you must remember to find a reason to
appreciate the warmth.

the ground beneath my feet

i've never really had anyone to count on.
i've always longed for someone to fight in
my corner. to tag me out when it became
too much. to stand over me when i am weak
and let me recover in the safety of their
strength. i've only ever had my own words,
my own thoughts, me. it's draining you
know, walking on sand. something so
willing to move from below you, despite
your body being confident to take each step.

what i forget is there are paths beside me to
my left and seas to float in to my right.
i must remember the fight is only alone, if
i do not seek the refuge of those
there to help.

J. R. Darbon

you have to understand that your actions do not define you unless you run from them. if you make a mistake, acknowledge it. own it. learn from it. apologise with sincerity and do not repeat it. people are too quick to try and escape from the repercussions, rather than learn the lesson. flowers won't blossom if you keep pulling them from the ground, fearful that people may think of them as a weed.

the ground beneath my feet

there are some things in this world that you may never truly get over and that's ok. there may still be a place in your heart for that boy from school or that girl you met on the beach. the love you had for 10 years may still sit somewhere in your heart, the same way the month-long fling still remains in the back of your mind. the key here is knowing that you loved, that you felt and appreciating that. each person that enters your heart becomes a part of your story, which is yours to feel, so feel it, all of it, feel every detail, if only in fleeting moments, feel them all.

J. R. Darbon

in a world so cold, you must stay warm. ice
won't last in the presence of fire,
remember this.

the ground beneath my feet

you cannot control the actions of another, and you won't always understand why they behave the way they do. but what you can control is the power you give them, how you react and the way you hold yourself. so, stand a little taller, breathe a little deeper and remind yourself exactly who you are, what you deserve and the value you hold in this world.

J. R. Darbon

there is so much beauty in self-discovery; understanding that being in love and loving yourself are not synonymous is so empowering. you are an infinite sky of stars on your own, you must always remember this.

the ground beneath my feet

really, the only way to assuage your mind is to rewrite your thoughts. to accept the feelings and change the narrative you give them. the rain may be dreary and cold, but you can seek solace in knowing that there is more pleasure in dancing in the storm, than there is in being afraid of it.

J. R. Darbon

you must lead by example,
if for nobody else,
then for yourself.

the ground beneath my feet

you really should care. you really should give a damn. you should be the person who loves, who tries, who answers messages, who reaches out even when you have been hurt. be the person you want those around you to be. if you're tired of games, do not play them. if you're wondering if they care, ask them. tell them all the reasons you do. everything you desire you should be putting out yourself. if you want happiness, start by giving. you will soon receive; the universe replicates your energy,
that i am sure of.

you are entitled to every emotion you feel. break, weep. allow the flood gates to open. release the emotions you feel unapologetically. unleash the anger you have inside safely. allow yourself to be empty. then, rebuild. pick yourself back up, find the joy in your life. learn what makes you happy, find what paints your face with a smile. remember that life is all about emotion, the good and the bad. feel them all, they are all part of who you are.

the ground beneath my feet

here's the thing, if you want to get it right, you have to learn from your past. acknowledge your mistakes, own them, appreciate the lessons and run forward with the momentum of change. nobody said you won't fall again, but the way you get back up says it all. finding yourself isn't easy, it might take longer than expected, but one day, each experience you've overcome will make perfect sense. trust the magic of the universe, believe in yourself and know that your future is yours to own, if only you harness it.

your life isn't on a time scale. people half your age might be married whilst people double that are happily single. owning a home does not mean you've made it any more than renting one. your career starting at 40 is just as much of an achievement as it would have been at 20. society tells us that we need to meet these norms, but none of us are the same. your journey is yours, nobody else's. stop comparing where you are to those around you, because you are not on the same path.

the ground beneath my feet

i cannot express how grateful i am that my life didn't turn out the way my younger self wished it did. those nights i'd long to be somebody that wasn't me, now a distant memory, the dream of marriage and property by twenty-five, the concept achieving it all by thirty. if i have learnt anything, it is that i want to live my life for me, for who i am, for who and what i want to be, not what others expect me to be. so, you can find me in the distant corners of my mind, exploring my individuality, finding adventure in the everyday, finding love in becoming precisely who i was meant to be.

J. R. Darbon

life isn't linear. it isn't this perfectly plotted grid of growth, leading from teenage love to marriage to being the boss of a company with a white picket fence and three kids. it's messy, it's scattered, it's raw and it's real. it has wild bouts of growth and sometimes plummets lower than predicted. some days it flatlines and that's okay. but i can promise you, the work you put in reflects the path you travel in the end. people say it's all okay in the end, but with a little self-love and a bit of guidance, the story of you ends up more than just okay, that i can promise you.

the ground beneath my feet

forget what you've been told, what your friends or family say. forget how society tells you to behave. act on how you feel, the way you think is right. do and say exactly what you believe in. no one changed the world by conforming to the standards set by everybody else. that's the thing with life, it doesn't always make sense. you are a juxtaposition of emotions, contradictory, yet perfectly blended.

there was a day, not too long ago when i stood before myself, candid, eyes wet with uncertainty. reflected upon the stained glass was somebody i wasn't entirely sure i knew. their features damaged, somewhat flawed, their rough skin drawing my eye. as my hand moved towards them, the cold connection of skin on glass sent the waves of realisation rushing through my veins. the inhale and exhale of a deep breath, the lock of eye contact with them reminded me who they were. they were strong, yet weak, fierce yet afraid. they were down, but certainly not out. they reminded me of everything i wanted to be, everything i wanted to be known for and everything i held close. they reminded me why i cared, why i loved and the chaos that had both hurt and healed me. but most importantly, without any words they reminded me that they love me. they resonated with me, as i continued to stare into their eyes. and it was in that moment i knew, i would never fear falling again.

the ground beneath my feet

and i could so easily have locked up my heart, but where would that leave me, but with hidden pain and nowhere to heal it. i held the broken fragments in my hands and pieced them back, one by one. my heart may no longer be in its original form, but believe me, it is more beautiful than it has ever been.

J. R. Darbon

as humans we are innately afraid of life, we remove ourselves emotionally from people, detaching from what is real. what i do not care for cannot hurt me; if i do not feel, i cannot experience pain. you ruin yourself by not loving, not caring. locking your heart up in shackles not only hides the love you have to give, but the love you will receive.

open your heart, remove the chains you have bound yourself to. the world might be tough, but so is your soul, without the armour you desperately cling onto. have the courage to let them in, for you are often safer swimming freely in the warm oceans of another, trusting your ability to float, than anchored down to the confines of an empty ship, afraid of what might be underneath.

the ground beneath my feet

with a soul that pure, the universe knew what to do with her. it waited, biding its time, evolving her ever more into the person she is today, simply to grant her perfectly with the purest love she could have ever desired, the kind only someone like her deserves. all this time she thought her story took a bit longer, when the universe knew it was only just beginning.

J. R. Darbon

there is something beautiful in the flaws we see, if only we look a little longer. the cracked glass at a family function that now has character, a story to tell. the charm of a small cottage covered in ivy, scaling the walls beautifully uninvited. the embrace of a loved one after a fight, when all is better again, a little tighter than it would normally be. life is all about perspective, so appreciate it all, the good, the bad and beautifully ugly.

the ground beneath my feet

do you know how much strength can be found in individuality, in knowing who you are, where you are from and where you are going. stand tall, breathe and remember who you are. you are the only person who has the ability to be you, to truly know you. and in that, you can find your power.

J. R. Darbon

i wish someone had told me it's okay to be me. that it was okay to love the same gender as me, that i could be feminine and masculine at the same time. i wish i hadn't spent three quarters of my life hiding who i was, afraid of how those who never truly knew me would feel. i wish i knew that half of my friends were feeling the same, not knowing they were hiding in the same closet i was, too scared of how we'd all feel about one another being different, when we are one and the same. i wish even once i'd found the strength to be who i am i didn't feel like i couldn't be open enough to express it. i wish i'd found my way sooner, i wish i knew how valuable i was. i wish i knew how much power there was in being me. i wish i'd known faster how many lives i'd change. i wish i realised quicker that who i am is everything i've always wanted to be. so, i hope you find the strength in these words to live for you, unapologetically and genuinely, because it's such a beautiful place to be.

the ground beneath my feet

to the boy who likes makeup and the girl who hates it, you can enjoy whatever you choose, you are valid, you are accepted, and you are beautiful. to the man who wants to cry but doesn't feel like he can and the woman whose tears are called weak, you are entitled to every ounce of emotion you feel, you are valid, you are accepted and you are beautiful. to the boy who likes boys, to the girl who likes girls, to those who like both, your sexuality does not define you, you are valid, you are accepted, and you are beautiful. to the person who doesn't feel right in their body, you know yourself better than anyone, you are valid, you are accepted, and you are beautiful. to the person reading this, to the people who feel different in any way, it is your life, live it how you wish without restraints, because you are valid, you are accepted and you are beautiful.

J. R. Darbon

and i'm not sorry. i'm not sorry that who i am, innately offends you. who people like me are. i'm not sorry that your fragile mind cannot comprehend that someone could be different, could be strong, could live in a way that defies the constraints society has placed upon us all. i'm not sorry that you don't understand the ignorance of your words, that you would rather see people like me die at the hands of hate than accept us to be part of a world that truly owns no place for the anger you hold towards us. and i'm not sorry that we celebrate who we are, because we fought for our right to sit at the same tables and we will be damned if we leave our seats, over the fragility of your weakness and self-doubts.

be alone. get to know yourself. spend time with your mind, with your thoughts, with you. if you are constantly requiring the presence of others, latching onto the validation that you are worthwhile from them, you will never truly achieve happiness. true recognition comes from within. when you sit with yourself, you find out who you are. you become your own best friend, candidly loving yourself for all that you are. and once you realise this, you'll never need authentication from others again.

J. R. Darbon

i don't care who you are, how old you are, where you are from or what you do, your life begins when you choose to live it for you, recklessly and shamelessly. when you decide to release yourself from the expectations of others, when you decide to live with vivacity. after all, there is no power in empty passion.

the ground beneath my feet

we all want love; we all want somebody to call us theirs and only theirs. but here's the thing, another person does not define us. we are whole all by ourselves. some things go perfectly together, the sun and the sea, the moon and the stars. but these are beautiful on their own, just like you.

J. R. Darbon

if you do anything today, please, stop thinking you need to have it all figured out. the inconsistency of life can be scary, but you must embrace it. some days you fall, others you rise, some you simply stand. you have no idea what tomorrow holds, yet you desperately assume that you should have it all together. breathe. take in the view. relax. it might not always be beautiful, but there's a story in every path you take. just know that you don't need to know what's coming next, to appreciate what you have right now.

the ground beneath my feet

wildflowers don't ask for permission to bloom, they just do. whether we want them to or not. you are a wildflower in your own story, unapologetically blossoming into the most beautiful version of you, there could be.

J. R. Darbon

life is not always synonymous, you can be happy and sad at the same time, strong and weak, settled and lost. but most of all, you can be you. chaos, peace and all.

the ground beneath my feet

sometimes you have to lose control to regain it. remove yourself from the chains in which you are ensnared with expectation and doubt. dance in the dimming light of the sunsets, revel in the down pours of rain, sing in the streets as if they were made of gold. but above all, live your life as if it was not yours to keep. because at the end of it all, it isn't. you won't get to live it again. live it; fully, each and every day.

J. R. Darbon

the more the world teaches me, the more i realise life was never about love, lust or adoration. nor was it about hate, vanity or power. it is everything in between, delicately mixed, hanging in the balance, aiding us to choose what we feel to be right, given the circumstances wider than our control. this is why we feel everything, to enable us to appreciate both the positive and the negative when they come, as well as when we need them.

the ground beneath my feet

just take a moment to appreciate where you
are now. breathe deeply. smile. you have
overcome every single thing you thought
would break you, ridden the waves of
change and embraced uncertainty. and you
will do this time and time again,
that i can assure you of.

J. R. Darbon

so, be love. be softness. be sincerity. be kindness. be adventure. be joy. be happiness. be everything you wish to find in the world. exude everything you long to find. because if you ever want to truly discover it, you'll have to first of all, look within yourself.

the ground beneath my feet

they held it all close. their thoughts and their mind. they took everything in their stride, step by step generating more and more power behind them. when the world tried to break them, they smiled and stood tall, time and time again. their heart was made of chaos, their soul full of desire. they were not somebody to take lightly, as they moved forward through time, each day stronger than the last. they didn't just know how to survive; they'd learnt how to live.

J. R. Darbon

i stood on the precipice and i jumped.
and all that was left of me were the doubts
i held about whether or not i could fly and
the ground beneath my feet.

the ground beneath my feet

J. R. Darbon

the ground beneath my feet

J. R. Darbon.

i wrote this book for me, for you, for us. i wrote this book to get everything out of me, to share my story, my life, my words, my thoughts, my soul. i hope this book finds you when you need it, i hope some of my words resonate with you. i hope you realise we all go through things, we all live, we all fall, we all rise. but most of all, i hope you and i never forget to be grateful for the journey, because if there is one thing i know, it's that you will always have the ground beneath your feet.

J. R. Darbon

the ground beneath my feet

this book is dedicated to everyone who
has ever made me feel anything.
thank you for the words.

J. R. Darbon

the ground beneath my feet

find me on Instagram
@jrdarbon
#jrdarbon

Printed in Great Britain
by Amazon